First published 2009 by Boxtree
an imprint of Pan Macmillan Ltd
Pan Macmillan, 20 New Wharf Road, London N1 9RR
Basingstoke and Oxford
Associated companies throughout the world
www.panmacmillan.com

ISBN 978-0-7522-2702-3

Text and illustrations © Modern Toss Limited 2009
PO Box 386, Brighton BN1 3SN, England
www.moderntoss.com

The right of Jon Link and Mick Bunnage to be identified as the
authors of this work has been asserted by them in accordance
with the Copyright, Designs and Patents Act 1988.

9 8 7 6 5 4 3 2 1

A CIP catalogue record for this book is available from
the British Library.

Designed and typeset by Modern Toss Limited
Printed by Proost, Belgium

Visit www.panmacmillan.com to read more about all our books and to buy them. You will also find features,
author interviews and news of any author events, and you can sign up for e-newsletters so that
you're always first to hear about our new releases.

all you can eat of

home~clubber

by Jon Link and Mick Bunnage

B⊞XTREE

home~clubber

a mobile phone company are paying me to hide this mast, I get free calls and I can cook bacon on it

home~clubber

I phoned up to complain about a cockroach on my pizza, turns out it's part of a 'Bush Tucker Trial' promotion. The bloke says if I eat it all he'll bike over a signed photo of Kilroy-Silk

home~clubber

following on from the success of the roast chicken flavoured crisp, this is a crisp flavoured chicken, perfect for the youth snack demographic

home~clubber

I've been on a traditional craft course learning how to write a letter with a pen and a piece of paper. All I've got to do now is scan it in and e-mail it to someone

home~clubber

the council are doing a special recycling Guy Fawkes night this year. You take all your old aerosol cans along and a safety officer lobs them on the fire for you

home~clubber

I got a text inviting me to a flash mob in a local car park. I was the only one who turned up, when I went home someone had cleared me flat out

home~clubber

thanks to an Arts Council loophole my mate's been able to set up his burger stall on the fourth plinth. It's gone so well he's been offered six months in the turbine hall at the Tate

home~clubber

Hello, is that Springwatch? Yeah I want to report having seen the first fly of summer

home~clubber

I'm lagging all my radiator pipes with goose fat and brandy butter from the January sales, it stops them from freezing up and gives off quite a nice seasonal aroma

home~clubber

following the success of the Somali pirates I've decided to start a highway robbery revival, I did a dry run on the meals on wheels van and managed to get a plate of curry out of it

home~clubber

have you ever tried sticking your tongue in a plug socket?

home~clubber

since I got this high-definition TV I've found I can't concentrate on Newsnight. Paxman's got a silver hair coming out of his nose that keeps catching the light

home~clubber

I'm taking part in an early 80's football hooligan re-enactment battle. It's all Arts Council funded so you get lunch and a free taxi back from the hospital

home~clubber

it's a mobile stair
security system,
burglars run up them
and knock themselves
out on the ceiling

home~clubber
I've developed this cigarette for smoking out of pub windows. I've trained my lungs to exhale all the smoke in one go when I'm outside stubbing it out

home~clubber
I've had a lot of stuff go missing since a keyhole surgeon moved in next door, it's mostly little things but if he starts operating through the letter box he could clear me out

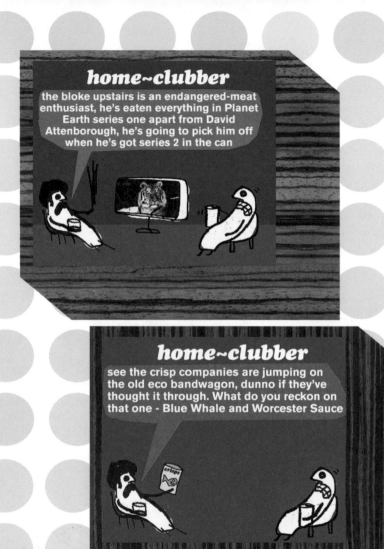

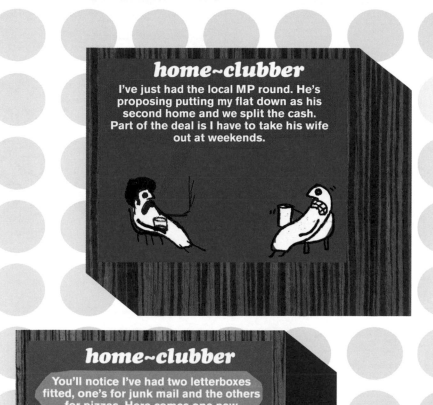

home~clubber

I'm living in a gambling hot spot, so I've adapted my front door to look like a fruit machine and people have started shoving money through the letter box

home~clubber

I've ordered 1/2 a ton of lettuce by accident from the supermarket home delivery, they're refusing to take it back but they have offered me a complimentary tube of mayonaise

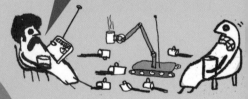

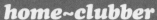

home~clubber

the local fried chicken shack have started
doing 'bring your own bird' nights.
If I catch this pigeon do you fancy eating
out tonight?

home~clubber

don't know if I'm going to do halloween
again, last night I had a herd of zombies
licking my door and asking for blankets,
turned out they forgot to lock the door in
the old people's home again

home~clubber

hello is that the Olympic Committee? Yeah some bloke claiming to carry your torch just asked to use my toilet, I think he forgot to pick it up on the way out

home~clubber

the local cafe have been selling pies with hairs in for years, since that film came out they've put their prices up and started calling them 'Sweeney Todds', this one's got a fingernail in as well

home~clubber

the local MP is offering a personalised recycling service, says he's mostly interested in receipts. He comes round on a Saturday morning with a big bin liner and does all the flats

home~clubber

I've had a chip put in my head so I can change channel, I'm having trouble keeping it off the adult movies at the moment

home~clubber

what d'you reckon?
it's the world's
most powerful
fridge magnet

home~clubber

this new wi-fi system I've had put
in is so powerful it's managed to
set fire to next door's curtains

home~clubber

they won't answer my calls about my busted toaster so I'm posting myself direct to the factory. I'm going to punch the first person who opens the box then try and talk them into mailing me back

home~clubber

I'd just finished watching that Ashes to Ashes, got up to make a cup of tea, fell over and banged my head, got time transported back one hour and had to watch it all again

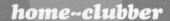

home~clubber

what do you reckon?
it's a video octopus,
I'm selling them down
the market, this one
used to be Top Gun

home~clubber

I've just had a short winter break, 10 days
at Sofa Village, picked this 2 seater up in
the sale and got a free lift home on it
in the back of the delivery van

home~clubber

I let the old lady upstairs make a call on my mobile, she took advantage and downloaded 800 quid's worth of Last Of The Summer Wine clips

home~clubber

I'm the only one in during the day so I have to sign for everyone's parcels. By way of a handling charge I'm reading through this lot before they come to collect them

home~clubber

welcome to my micro fish farm system, I put an egg in the first tank and move it along as it gets bigger. This one's ready to eat

home~clubber

I've extended my flat out into the street, builder reckoned I didn't need planning permission. All going well until this bus ploughed into it

home~clubber

I've been researching my family tree on the internet, so far all I've found is a photo of my sister naked with a lorry driver

home~clubber

I've had this camera installed, I've got a feeling that upstairs have started fly-tipping again

home~clubber

I've got a job as his dog walker, but unless I let him watch telly and give him half the money he says he'll get me sacked

home~clubber

I might have to move that fridge a bit, I've accidentally worn a ritual footpath in the carpet

home~clubber

the government are cracking down on the parents of fat kids. If I can put on 3 stone I reckon I can get my old man banged up for Christmas, at least it's warm in there

last year I got it the wrong way round and someone nicked my stereo

home~clubber

I've been sucking all the preservative air out of this pre-packaged food, so far I've added about five years on my life

home~clubber

the local chippy's got a closing down sale on, everything must go. What d'you reckon on this, boil-in-the-bowl goldfish and chips?

home~clubber

hello is that the council? Yeah I think someone might have stolen my identity and paid my council tax bill by mistake, how do I go about getting it back?

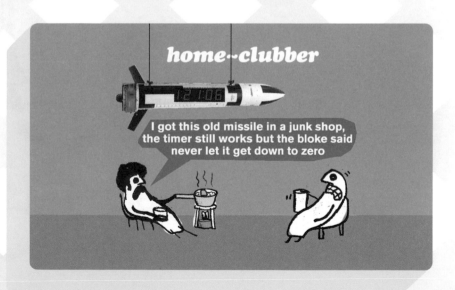

home~clubber

I've been headhunted for the first space trip to Mars, it's about a year there and a year back, mainly involves sitting in a chair and answering the phone. I'm down for team leader

it's the world's first all-format entertainment pod, I'm currently watching someone read an audio book on video

home~clubber

I've been getting a lot of unwanted guests lately, so I've installed this armchair meter, if they overstay their welcome I fine them 30 quid

home~clubber

I've just bought this 40 litre wall-mounted sauce bottle, according to the sell-by date I've got 3 years to eat it, do you fancy a bit of sauce on toast?

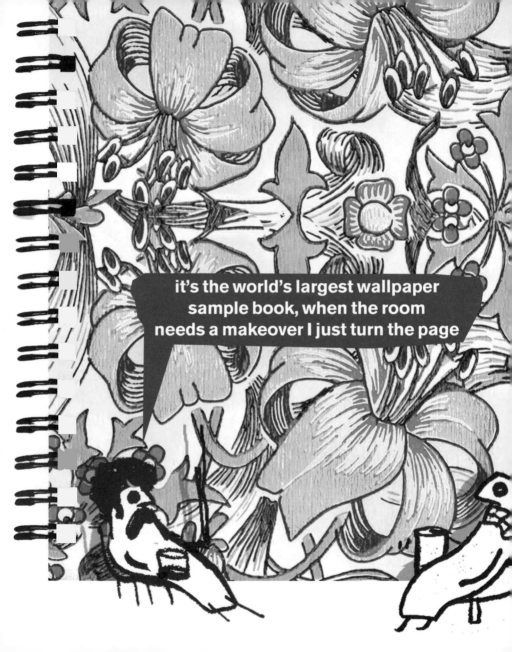

home~clubber

my acupuncturist reckons I might have over-stimulated a hair gland when I sat on a pin

home~clubber

I got everyone in the block to stick their wine dregs in this wheelie bin. The radiator's heated it up nicely I just need to fling in another kebab to tweak the spice level

home~clubber

I couldn't be bothered with my window box anymore, so I had it concreted over

home~clubber

after the success of my window-baked chicken I've stepped up production using this washing line, whack a bit more suncream on that big 'un?

home~clubber

I've been filming myself eating food and then posting it on youtube. So far 47,000 people have said they like it and one person has threatened to kill me, apparently that's not bad

home~clubber

X Factor auditions are on down the shopping centre later on, I'm going to be showcasing my talent for knocking back a bottle of gin in 15 seconds

home~clubber

this jewellery is made out of the most
expensive substance know to man,
solidified balls of printer ink

home~clubber

when I agreed to sponsor a bear at
the zoo I didn't realise he was doing a
burger eating contest for leukaemia research

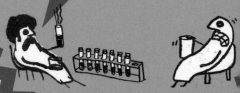

home~clubber

It's an old shaman method - hurts a
bit at first but once the endorphins
kick in you're on a 24 hour high

home~clubber

this virtual holiday is a welcome break, I'm on a cruise at the moment watching Sky News in my cabin, wack some of this oil on my back I might go up on deck in a bit

home~clubber

what you're looking at there, is a WW2 tree sharpener, burn all the leaves off, then sharpen the top to a point, lethal to a parachutist

home~clubber

I've installed a CCTV camera, to see if I really did smash that wall through in my sleep

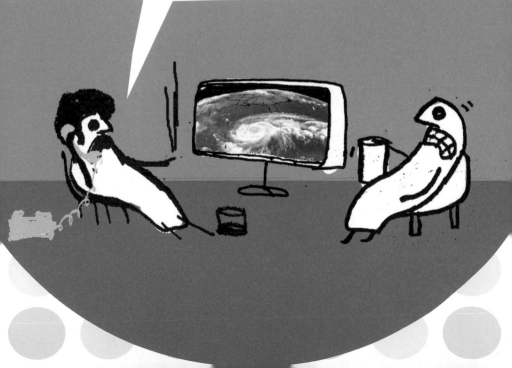

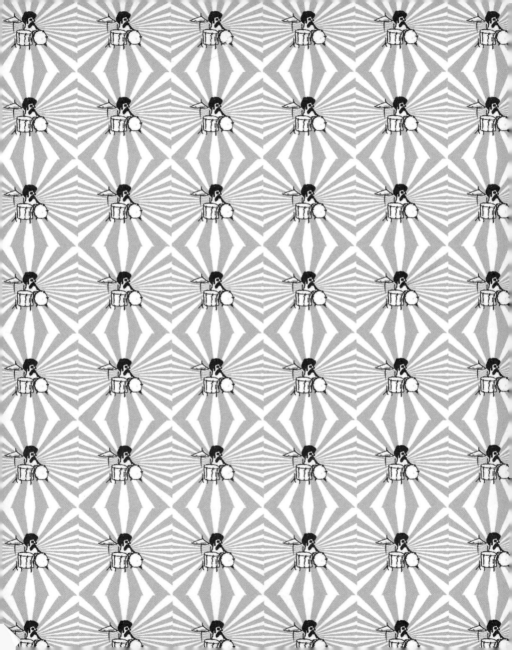